Food

Ashley Lee

e Explore other books at:
WWW.ENGAGEBOOKS.COM

VANCOUVER, B.C.

e→ WWW.ENGAGEBOOKS.COM

Food: Level 2
I Can Help Save Earth!
Lee, Ashley 1995 –
Text © 2020 Engage Books
Design © 2020 Engage Books

Edited by: A.R. Roumanis

Text set in Arial Regular.
Chapter headings set in Arial Black.

FIRST EDITION / FIRST PRINTING

LIBRARY AND ARCHIVES CANADA CATALOGUING IN PUBLICATION

Title: Food: I Can Help Save Earth Level 2
Names: Lee, Ashley, 1995- author

Identifiers: Canadiana (print) 20200309803 | Canadiana (ebook) 20200309811
ISBN 978-1-77437-727-7 (hardcover)
ISBN 978-1-77437-728-4 (softcover)
ISBN 978-1-77437-729-1 (pdf)
ISBN 978-1-77437-730-7 (epub)
ISBN 978-1-77437-731-4 (kindle)

Subjects:
LCSH: Food—Environmental aspects—Juvenile literature
LCSH: Food waste—Environmental aspects—Juvenile literature
LCSH: Food habits—Environmental aspects—Juvenile literature
LCSH: Agriculture—Environmental aspects—Juvenile literature
LCSH: Environmental protection—Citizen participation—Juvenile literature

Classification: LCC QL668.E2 L44 2020 | DDC J597.8/9—DC23

Contents

What is Farming?

Farming is when people grow plants or raise animals for food.

Some farms only grow plants.
Others only raise animals.
Some farms do both.

How is Food Made?

Farms send plants and animals to factories to be cleaned, preserved, and packaged for people to eat.

KEY WORD

Preserved: a process of treating food to keep it from going bad quickly.

Bread is made from flour. Flour comes from a plant called wheat. Wheat has to be ground into a fine powder before it can be used for bread.

Why Are Farms Important?

Many people live in cities where they cannot grow their own food. They need to buy food from farms.

Farming creates jobs for about 1 in 7 people on Earth. This includes people who grow, collect, clean, and package food.

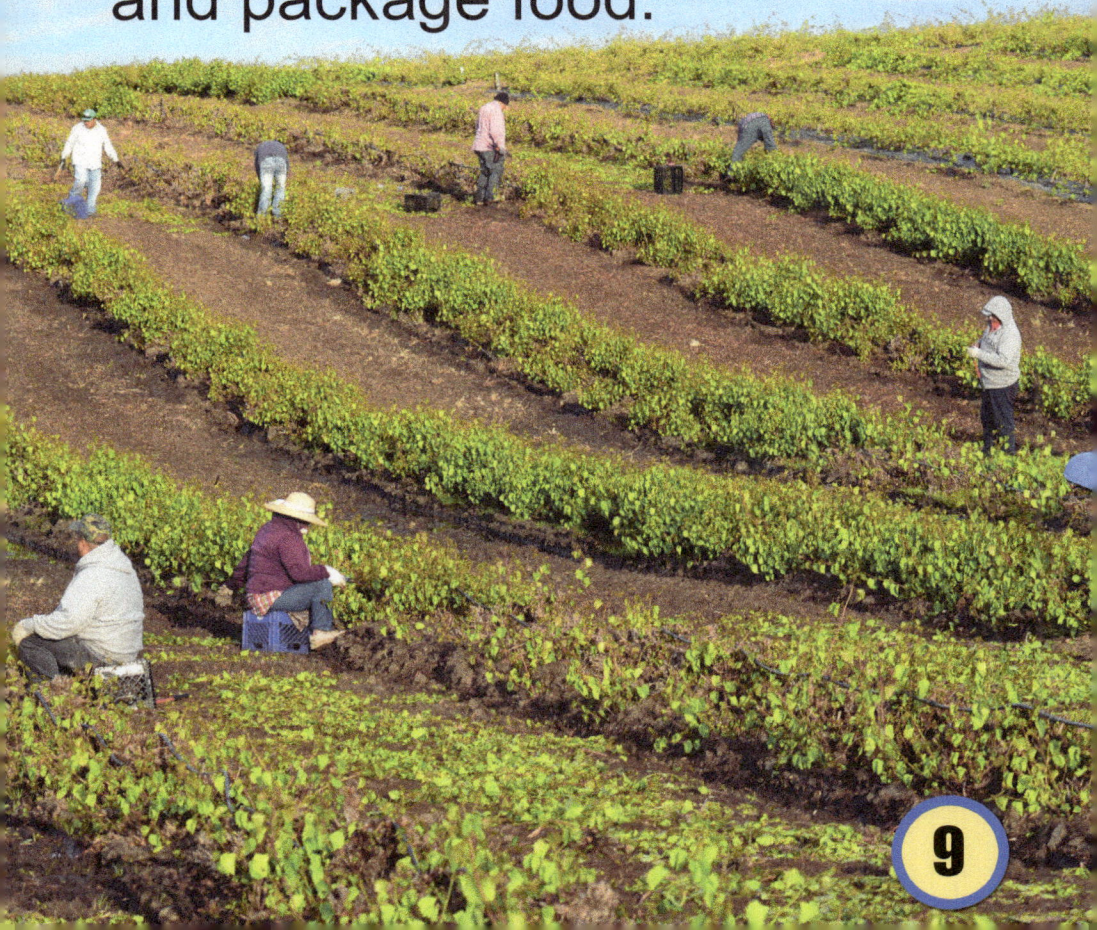

Farming Around the World

Many fruits and vegetables are grown in places with warm weather. They are then sent to other countries. Pigs, cows, and chickens are the most common animals raised on farms.

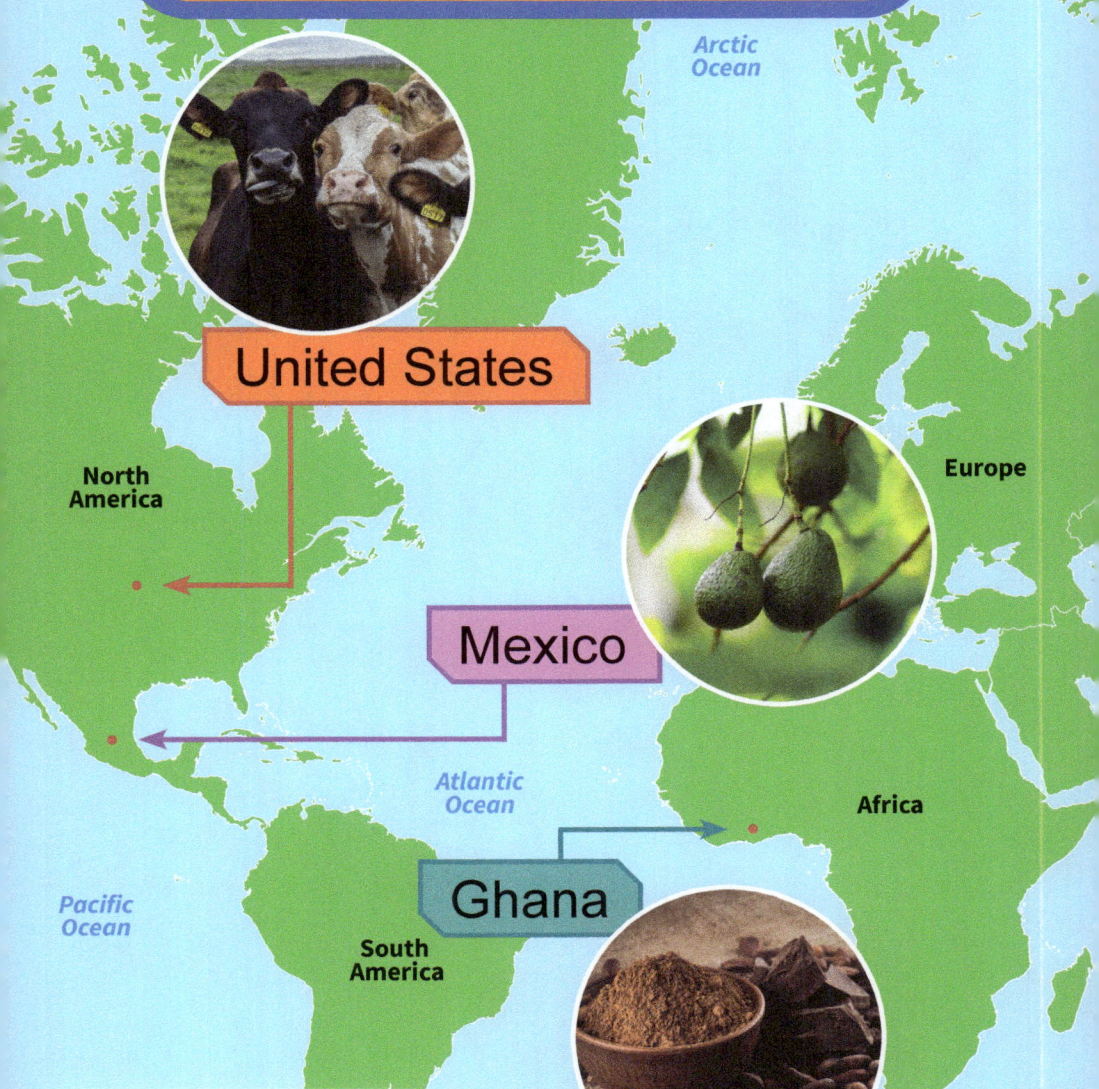

The United States raises more cows for beef than any other country. Ghana grows the most cocoa to make chocolate. Mexico is known for growing avacados.

Arctic Ocean

United States

North America

Europe

Mexico

Atlantic Ocean

Africa

Pacific Ocean

South America

Ghana

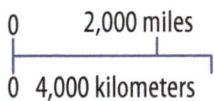

0   2,000 miles

0   4,000 kilometers

N

Legend
Land
Ocean

11

How Do Farms Cause Pollution?

Pesticides are chemicals that keep bugs away from food. Chemical fertilizers help plants grow bigger. Both pesticides and chemical fertilizers can enter the ground and find their way into rivers and oceans.

Cows, sheep, and goats all burp methane gas. Methane gas pollutes the air. Waste from farm animals can pollute water sources.

13

Is All Farming Harmful?

Organic farms are farms that use natural methods to keep plants healthy. Instead of using pesticides, some organic farms use ladybugs. Ladybugs will eat other insects without harming plants.

These farms also use manure or kitchen scraps as fertilizer. This means they do not have to use chemical fertilizers.

15

Farming Pollution Facts

Farm animals in the United States create about 500 million tons (508 million metric tons) of waste every year.

About 5.6 billion pounds (2.5 billion kilograms) of pesticides are used around the world every year.

About 10 billion farm animals are raised in the United States every year.

Every year 40 million tons (41 million metric tons) of harmful gasses are released into the air when making chemical fertilizers.

Water sources that are polluted by animal waste contain more than 40 different diseases that can harm people.

About 260 million acres of forests in the United States have been destroyed to grow food for farm animals.

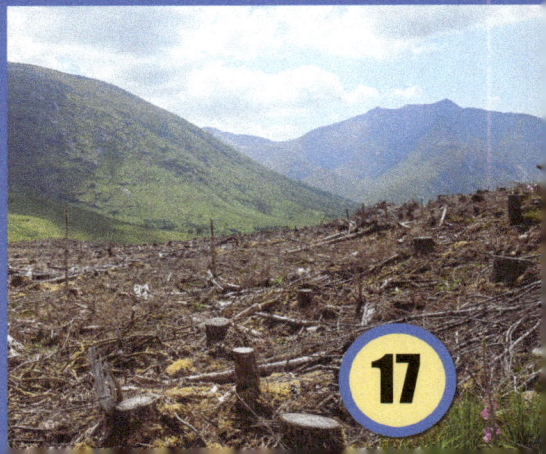

How Farming Pollution Affects Animals

When chemical fertilizers end up in water sources, they make a plant called algae grow quickly. Algae takes oxygen out of the water.

KEY WORD

Oxygen: a chemical that all life breathes to survive.

Fish need oxygen to breathe. Too much algae growth kills fish and other water animals.

How Farming Pollution Affects Humans

An antibiotic is a medicine that stops infections. Some farms give animals antibiotics to make them bigger. Antibiotics can be transferred to humans when they eat meat. People can become **immune** to antibiotics when they have a lot of them. This means that antibiotics will not heal their infections.

KEY WORD

Immune: when a medicine or illness cannot affect a person's body.

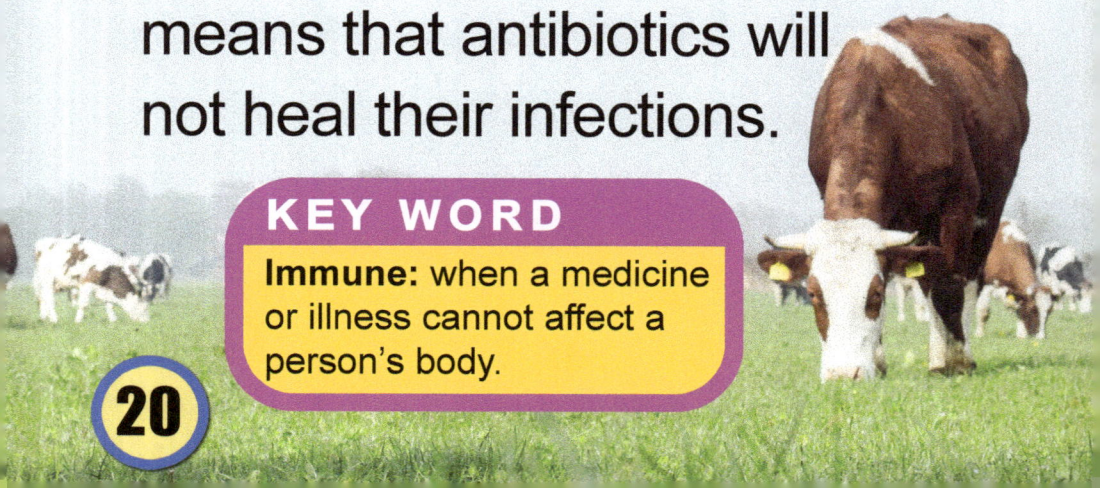

People can breathe in pesticides when they are sprayed on plants. Pesticides can also stay on fruits and vegetables after they are picked. People can become sick if they eat or breathe in pesticides.

21

How Farming Pollution Affects Earth

Methane gas made by farm animals is one of the causes of global warming. Global warming means Earth's temperature is rising. This happens when chemicals become trapped in Earth's **atmosphere**. Global warming can cause strong storms and wildfires.

KEY WORD

Atmosphere: a layer of gas that surrounds Earth. It provides air for living things to breathe.

Trees provide oxygen for all living things to survive. Many forests have been destroyed to make room for farms. The more meat people eat, the more land is needed to raise farm animals and grow food for them.

Food Waste and Composting

About 1.3 billion tons (1.32 billion metric tons) of food are thrown away around the world every year. Food waste can end up in landfills where it is buried. When food is buried it does not have access to air.

Food needs air to break down properly. Buried food without air creates methane gas. Many people are starting to compost at home. They are able to make sure the compost has access to air.

Reducing Farming Pollution

Shoppers are becoming more aware of how farming is affecting Earth. This has led many farms to stop using pesticides and chemical fertilizers.

Many people are reducing food waste by making donations to food banks and homeless shelters.

DONATION BOX

27

The Future of Farming

More people are starting to buy food from organic farms. This lets large farms know that people do not want pesticides or chemical fertilizers used on their food.

Many people are eating less meat. They hope that less farm animals will need to be raised for food.

Quiz

Test your knowledge of food by answering the following questions. The questions are based on what you have read in this book. The answers are listed on the bottom of the next page.

1 What are the most common animals raised on farms?

2 What are pesticides?

3 What are organic farms?

4 What has been destroyed to make room for farms?

5 How much food is thrown away around the world every year?

6 Why are many people eating less meat?

Explore other level 2 readers.

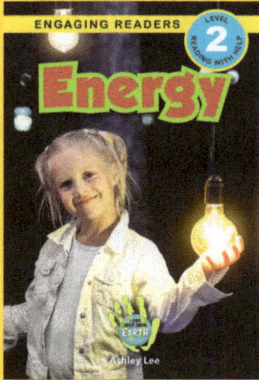
ENGAGING READERS — LEVEL 2 — Energy — Ashley Lee

ENGAGING READERS — LEVEL 2 — Food — Ashley Lee

ENGAGING READERS — LEVEL 2 — Goods — Ashley Lee

ENGAGING READERS — LEVEL 2 — Plastics — Ashley Lee

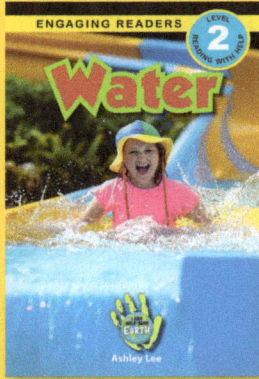
ENGAGING READERS — LEVEL 2 — Water — Ashley Lee

ENGAGING READERS — LEVEL 2 — Butterflies — Ashley Lee

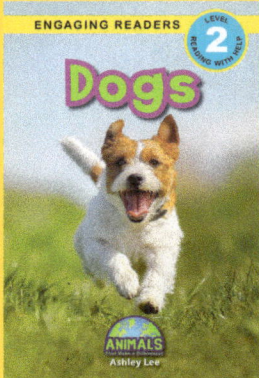
ENGAGING READERS — LEVEL 2 — Dogs — Ashley Lee

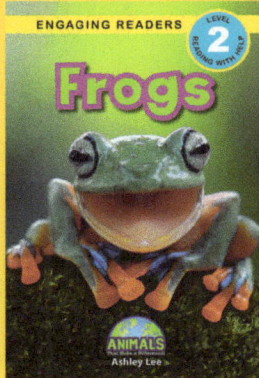
ENGAGING READERS — LEVEL 2 — Frogs — Ashley Lee

ENGAGING READERS — LEVEL 2 — Primates — Ashley Lee

Visit www.engagebooks.com to explore more Engaging Readers.

Answers: 1. Pigs, cows, and chickens 2. Chemicals that keep bugs away from food 3. Farms that use natural methods to keep plants healthy 4. Forests 5. About 1.3 billion tons (1.32 metric tons) 6. They hope that less farm animals will need to be raised for food

31

www.ingramcontent.com/pod-product-compliance
Lightning Source LLC
Chambersburg PA
CBHW051236020426
42331CB00016B/3399